The Story of Noah and the Rainbow

Patricia A. Pingry

Illustrated by Stacy Venturi-Pickett

A Word to Parents and Friends

This story is one of a series of biblical stories especially written, illustrated, and designed to explain a difficult concept in a gentle and simple manner.

Even the youngest child will understand the timeless lesson inherent in each bible story. Most of all, preschoolers, beginning readers, and older children will enjoy hearing and reading these exciting accounts of heroes from one of the oldest and most exciting books of all: the Holy Bible.

Ideals Publishing Corporation
Nashville, Tennessee

ISBN 0-8249-8176-6

Once upon a time, not long after the beginning of time, there were no rainbows. There were people and animals and water and flowers. But there were no rainbows. There were deserts and camels and palm trees. But there were no rainbows.

Out in the desert lived an old man named Noah. He was *very* old—600 years old! One day, God talked to Noah. God told Noah to build a boat. A big boat. A boat called an ark.

Noah was to build the ark from wood and cover it with tar so that it would float.

Noah listened to God and started to build the ark. He made the rooms just as God told him to make them.

Noah's ark would have three decks. The lower deck had a room big enough for two baby elephants and a room high enough for two baby giraffes.

On the middle deck were rooms for colts to run back and forth and monkeys to swing.

On the upper deck, Noah built some little rooms which were as tiny as nests. Noah lined those rooms with leaves and twigs.

While Noah was building the ark, his neighbors passed by on their camels.

"Old Noah is just wasting his time," they said, "trying to build a boat in the desert."

Then they said, "Old Noah is foolish."

Finally they said, "Old Noah is crazy!"

Noah kept building his ark. When he finished, he began carrying in leaves and grass and dates and figs. He put some of these in almost every room. Noah also built platforms in some rooms and ladders in others. He made a soft bed in each room.

God had told Noah he would send animals to the ark, a male and a female of every kind of animal on earth. God had also told Noah that the people on earth were very bad and he was sorry he had made them. God told Noah that he would send enough water to drown every living thing. Only those animals in the ark and Noah and his family, whom God loved, would be safe.

And as Noah was finishing the rooms and the nests, young animals began arriving at the ark. Two baby elephants came lumbering up, a girl and a boy, and Old Noah showed them where they could sleep. Two young leopards raced to Noah's door and he showed them to their room.

Two by two, male and female, animals from all over the earth came to Noah's ark. Huge pythons from India slithered up the ramp. Brilliantly colored peacocks strutted to the door. Fuzzy white polar bears huffed and puffed in the heat. Squalling hyenas arrived in the desert. Mice and rats and guinea pigs and gerbils raced back and forth, scurrying by Old Noah. Lambs bleated and frolicked with mewing lion cubs.

At long last, every animal was inside the ark with Noah and his family. On that day, the Lord shut the door.

Noah walked through the upper deck and saw that ravens and sparrows and ostriches and monkeys were all there. They were chirping and squealing and climbing and fighting.

On the middle deck, the calves and the ponies and baby zebras were kicking and neighing. The young panthers were racing around their room and rolling over the leopards.

In the lower rooms, the elephants began trumpeting. The donkeys were braying, the rattlesnakes were quietly coiled.

And Noah wondered, just for a moment, if he might be crazy after all. But then it began to rain.

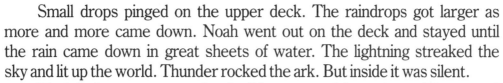

Small drops pinged on the upper deck. The raindrops got larger as more and more came down. Noah went out on the deck and stayed until the rain came down in great sheets of water. The lightning streaked the sky and lit up the world. Thunder rocked the ark. But inside it was silent.

Noah had never seen such rain. Water poured from above. The ground split and water spewed up from inside the earth. Then Noah knew he was not crazy. Noah knew God was destroying all life on earth. Only what was in the ark would be safe. And Noah was not scared.

The water grew deeper and deeper. At last the ark began to float. The water covered Noah's old house. It rose higher than the treetops. The water covered the mountaintops. For forty days and forty nights, the rain came down, the water rose, and the ark drifted.

One morning, Noah awoke and it was quiet. The thunder had stopped, and there were no raindrops on the roof. The rain had stopped, and the wind was gently blowing. Soon Noah could see the tops of the mountains again.

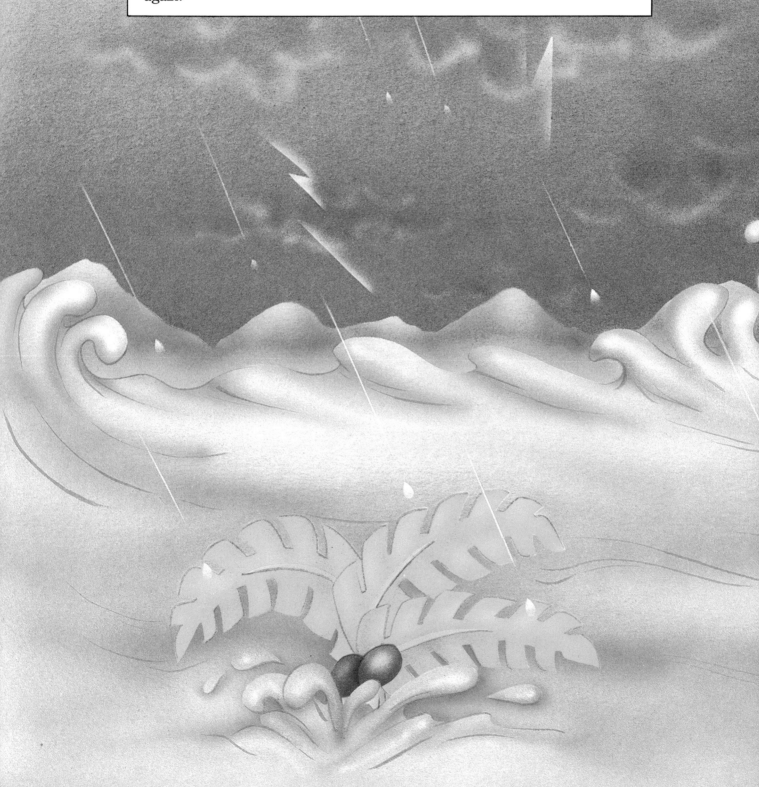

One day, Noah went to the deck. He gently picked up a white dove and lifted her to the sky. The dove flew out of sight. After an hour or so, she returned to Noah carrying a small olive branch. Noah knew that the water was now below the treetops.

Noah waited a week. Then he let two doves fly away, and this time they did not return. Noah knew that the water was below the tree branches.

Noah still waited until, finally, all the water was gone. He opened the door to the ark and stepped outside. How good it felt to stand on solid ground again!

The animals followed. Two by two, male and female of each type of animal on the earth came out of the ark. They were a little bigger by now, and not quite as frisky.

When the ark was empty, Noah and his family knelt on the dry ground. They thanked God for keeping them safe. They thanked God for a beautiful clean world in which to live.

Soon the animals left Noah and the ark and started to find their own new homes.

As they left, Noah looked up and saw wonderful colors in the clean sky. And God again talked to Noah. He said, "This is my rainbow which I have set in the sky. Now, when it rains, you will see my rainbow and you shall know that never again will I destroy the world with water."

The rainbow is God's promise of his love.